JENSEN
CARS

ISBN 978-1-7398450-9-4

Acknowledgements

Our thanks to Derek Chapman and to Cropredy Bridge Garage for allowing us to photograph their cars. Additional thanks to Titty Ho Motor Company who provided the Jensen Interceptor Convertible that appears in this book and to Tony Banham of Jensen International Automotive.

Picture Credits

The majority of the photographs in this book are those of the author

Distributed in the U. S. A. by:
SCB Distributors,
15608 South New Century Drive,
Gardena, CA 90248,
U. S. A.

Other Titles by CP Press

Essential Aston Martin DB7, DB9, DB11

Bentley Continental

Lotus Cortina and Elan

The similarity in style between the Austin A40 Sports and the original 1950's Jensen Interceptor was no coincidence. The Jensens wanted to produce a sports-touring car using Austin components. Leonard Lord wanted Jensen to design and build a car for Austin. Eric Neale who had joined Jensen as a designer in 1946 submitted several designs and the A40 Sports - Tourer was essentially a smaller Jensen Interceptor. The Jensen Interceptor actually arrived a year before the Austin A40 Sports. The Jensen Interceptor was launched at The London Motor Show in 1949. It's body was the work of Jensen's Chief Engineer, Eric Neale - who used a lengthened A70 chassis as the platform. The Jensen Interceptor had a 4 litre, six cylinder Austin Sheerline engine. The Jensen Interceptor of 1950 could achieve 100mph and 0-60mph in thirteen seconds. The Jensen Interceptor was available as a fixed head coupe or a convertible. The convertible Interceptor had a rigid Perspex rear and three-quarter windows that sank into the car's body when lowering the hood.

This particular car was owned by Lord Strathcarron, the man who came up with the Jensen Interceptor name. The convertible Interceptor is seen here with the roof up.

This car is registered MXM 979 and is a 1952 model.

The original 1950's Jensen Interceptor used a lengthened A70 chassis with the centre portion of the cruciform lowered to reduce the car's height.

Jensen Interceptor Cabriolet Specifications	
Capacity:	3993 cc
Bore:	87 millimetres
Stroke:	111 millimetres
Valves:	ohv push rod
Compression Ratio:	6.8 to 1
Maximum Power:	130bhp
Maximum Torque:	212 lb ft @ 2200 rpm

Austin badge, confirming that the early Jensen Interceptor used the same engine from the Austin Sheerline.

First Austin Sheerline cars had a 3460cc straight six overhead valve engine, but this was quickly increased to a 3993cc engine seen here.

With the 3993cc engine the designation became A125 Sheerline. The engine is seen here in the Jensen Interceptor.

Vent on the bonnet shows this to be an early Jensen Interceptor.

The Jensen badge that is on the grill.

Production 1950 - 1957
32 Jensen Interceptor Convertibles
52 Jensen Interceptor Coupes
4 Jensen Interceptor Sedancas
88 cars produced from 1950 to 1957

On 17 October 1956 The Motor magazine stated: "The unique distinction of being the first British Company to market a production saloon fitted with disc brakes to all four wheels has been achieved by Jensen Motors Ltd with the introduction of a deluxe version of the Jensen 541 for it is equipped thoughout with the latest version of the Dunlop disc brakes."

Eric Neale had suggested 531 as the name of the car and this was almost accepted but Richard Jensen changed it to 541 as the coming new model year would be 1954. The prototype was registered JEA 541.

The new Jensen C-V8 was introduced on the Earl's Court stand in October 1962. Twelve months after the introduction of the C-V8 the Mark II model was announced with numerous detail revisions. Chassis number 104/2230 was the car finished by Hardy Amies and was registered EHA1. A Jensen C-V8 registered HEA 5D was presented to Richard Jensen on his retirement from the company.

Work on this unique Jensen C-V8 Coupe cabriolet started in June 1964. The wheelbase was increased by nine inches to provide extra space behind the rear seats to house the folded down hood when in open-top position.

The Jensen P66 is the sole survivor of two prototypes that were built in the mid-1960's. It was the last car ever built under the control of the Jensen Brothers and the last to be produced by designer Eric Neale.

It was possibly conceived as the proposed Jensen Interceptor but at the time Jensen was being handed over to the Norcos Group and Kevin Beattie got Touring Superleggera of Milan to design the car that has become the familiar Jensen Interceptor.

Jensen badge on the P66

Note the 'J' in the middle of the sidelights.

The Jensen P66 was displayed at the 1965 London Motor Show.

Had the Jensen P66 gone into production it would have delayed the launch of a CV-8 replacement.

Superb vinyl interior of the Jensen P66

The 6276cc V8 engine.

Instrument binnacles face the driver.

Accessing the spare wheel is made easy.

It is believed that when the decision was made not to go ahead with the Jensen P66 prototype Alan Jensen gave the instruction to break up both cars. The hardtop avoided this fate as it was not in the factory.

A close-up of the front lights of the P66.

Owner Derek Chapman had a windscreen specially made for this car.

Metal plate confirms chassis number JM EXP112 and that this was an experimental car.

The Vignale Prototype

In early 1966 a Jensen CV8 was sent to Vignale Carrozzeria, where its fibreglass body was taken off and replaced with steel Jensen Interceptor panels. Later in 1966, the first consignment of Vignale bodies arrived at the West Bromwich factory and the Jensen Interceptor FF were ready for the 1966 Earl's Court Show in 1966.

The prototype Jensen Interceptor did not have a regular chassis number, in fact it had chassis number EXP 115 and was registered HEA ID. This prototype also did not have power-steering, its automatic shift did not have a "park" position and it had walnut veneer on the door trims. The fact that it had chassis number EXP 115 meant that it was an experimental vehicle. The arrangement between Jensen Motors and Vignale was short-lived ending in 1967 after just 50 cars. The jigs and machine tools were brought back to West Bromwich.

Vignale produced prototype bodies for Rolls Royce and Fiat but perhaps they were best known for the Maserati 3500 sports car that was built between 1960 and 1962.

Beattie gave Vignale the original designs for the Interceptor which had been done in the Touring studios, and Vignale adapted them.

This is the first production Interceptor. Built on experimental chassis JM/EXP115, the car was later given chassis number 115/2495.

EXP/115 was registered as a demonstrator and promotional vehicle on 10 September 1966.

Performance

ACCELERATION

True speed mph	Time in secs	Car Speedo mph
30	3.3	30
40	4.3	40
50	5.9	50
60	7.3	60
70	9.5	70
80	12.1	80
90	15.4	90
100	19.0	99
110	24.9	109
120	32.2	117

Standing ¼ mile
15.7 sec 92 mph

Standing kilometre
28.4 sec 115 mph

Mileage recorder:
2 per cent under-reading

TEST CONDITIONS

Weather	Drizzle
Wind	3-8 mph
Temperature	7 deg C (44 deg F)

MAXIMUM SPEED

Gear	mph	kph	rpm
Top (mean)	133	214	5100
(best)	133	214	5100
Inter	92	148	5100
Low	54	87	5100

BRAKES

FADE (from 30 mph in neutral)

Load	g	Distance
25 lb	20%	150 ft
50 lb	40%	75 ft
75 lb	60%	50 ft
100 lb	85%	35 ft
125 lb	90%	33.4 ft
Handbrake	35%	000 ft

GEAR RATIOS AND TIME IN SEC

mph	Top (3.07 – 6.75)	Inter (4.44 – 9.77)	Low (7.50 – 16.5)
10-30	-	3.0	2.1
20-40	4.4	3.3	2.4
30-50	4.5	3.9	2.7
40-60	5.1	3.5	-
50-70	5.9	3.9	-
60-80	6.1	5.1	-
70-90	6.4	6.1	-
80-100	8.0	-	-
90-110	9.5	-	-
100-120	12.2	-	-

FUEL CONSUMPTION

(at constant speed – mpg)

30 mph	25.8
40 mph	24.5
50 mph	22.3
60 mph	20.6
70 mph	18.7
80 mph	15.8
90 mph	14.9
100 mph	12.8

Typical mpg 14.2 (19.9 litres/100 km)
Overall mpg 13.6 (20.8 litres/100 km)

TURNING CIRCLES

Between kerbs
L, 36 ft 7 in.; R, 38 ft 5 in.
Between walls
L, 38 ft 3 in.; R, 40 ft 1 in.
Steering wheel turns, lock to lock 3.5

WEIGHT

Kerb weight 33.0 cwt (3697 lb – 1680 kg)
(with oil, water and half-full fuel tank)
Distribution per cent:
F, 50.0; R, 50.0
Laden as tested:
35.3 cwt (3947 lb – 1794 kg)

In October 1968 at Earl's Court the MKI Interceptor was launched. The design was originally by Vignale and Touring Superleggera. It was completed by Eric Neale at Jensen.

Specification

Front Engine, Rear-Wheel Drive

ENGINE	
Cylinders	8, in 90 degree vee
Cooling system	Water; pump, thermostat and twin electric fans
Bore	108 mm (4.25 in)
Stroke	86 mm (3.38 in)
Displacement	6,276 cc (383 cu in)
Valve gear	Overhead, hydraulic tappets
Compression ratio	10-to-1
Carburettors	Carter 4-barrel progressive
Fuel pump	Mechanical
Oil filter	Full-flow, renewable element
Max. power	325 bhp (gross) at 4,600 rpm
Max. torque	425 lb ft (gross) at 2,800 rpm
TRANSMISSION	
Gearbox	Torque Flite Hi-performance, 3-speed automatic with torque converter
Gear ratios	Top 1.0-2.2; Inter 1.44-3.19; Low 2.44-5.39; Reverse 2.19-4.91
Final drive	Hypoid bevel with Powr-Lok limited slip differential, 3.07 to 1
CHASSIS and BODY	
Construction	Steel body and tubular frame welded together
SUSPENSION	
Front	Independent, twin coil springs, wishbones, lever-arm dampers, anti-roll bar
Rear	Live axle, dual-rate half-elliptic leaf springs, Panhard rod, telescopic Armstrong Selectaride dampers
STEERING	
Type	Cam gears, rack and pinion
Wheel diameter	17 in
BRAKES	
Make and type	Dunlop discs front and rear, divided circuit
Servo	Vacuum type
Dimensions	F 11.25 in dia; R 11.25 in dia
Swept area	F 249.1 sq in; R 249.1 sq in. Total 498.2 sq in (282 sq in per laden ton)
WHEELS	
Type	Pressed steel disc, chrome plated and pierced, 4.5 in wide rim
Tyres – make	Dunlop
- type	RS.5 tubed cross-ply
- size	6.70-15 in
EQUIPMENT	
Battery	12-volt 72-amp hr.
Alternator	40 amp
Headlamps	4 Lucas sealed beam 37.5/50 watt
Reversing lamps	2
Electric fuses	5
Screen wipers	2-speed, self-parking
Screen washer	Standard electric
Interior heater	Standard, water-valve control
Safety belts	Standard in front
Interior trim	Leather seats, pvc headlining
Floor covering	Wilton carpet
Windscreen	Laminated
Starting handle	No provision
Jack	Bevelift
Jacking points	4, 2 each side
Underbody protection	Bitumastic on all surfaces exposed to road
Other bodies	None
MAINTENANCE	
Fuel tank	16 Imp gallons (low level warning lamp) (73 litres)
Cooling system	32 pints (including heater) (18.2 lts)
Engine sump	8.5 pints (4.7 litres) SAE 20W/40. Change oil every 4,000 miles. Change filter every 8,000 miles
Gearbox	17 pints SAE ATF Type A. No change
Final drive	3 pints Shell Limited Slip diff. S6721A. Change oil every 12,000 miles
Grease	6 points every 1,000 miles. 4 points every 4,000 miles.
Tyre pressures	F 24; R 28 psi

The Jensen Interceptor Series II was introduced in October 1969.

Jensen Interceptor II

Following successful use of the Chrysler V8 5.9-litre engine in the C-V8, Jensen used the basically similar unit in its larger 6,276cc form for the new Interceptor launched in October 1966. The sleek new body was built in steel by Touring to Vignale patents and represented a breakaway from the glass fibre construction used for the C-V8. A sturdy tubular chassis was retained, welded to the steel body, and the car was available initially with either automatic or manual transmission. When tested in 1967 it gave a maximum speed of 133 mph. Power assisted steering became first available, then standard, from January 1969.

In October 1969 the Series II Interceptor was introduced, having Dunlop SP Sport tyres, a larger radiator, and air-conditioning as an optional extra at £220. The fuel capacity was increased to 20 gallons and, externally, black headlamp surrounds, new bumpers, overriders and side grilles identified the new car. The example tested was one of the early Series II Interceptors produced. In this form the Interceptor continued for two years, until replaced by the Interceptor III, having ventilated disc brakes, cast aluminium wheels, and remote locking for the passenger door. Finally, the bore and stroke of the V8 engine were increased to give a capacity of 7,212 cc and this was introduced on Interceptor production from chassis number 4643 in May 1972.

Jensen Interceptor II 1969 - 1971		
Chassis Series	**Type**	**Numbers Built**
123	RHD Automatic	694
125	LHD Automatic	432
EXP	Experimental Cars	2
	TOTAL	**1128**

Jensen Interceptor III Convertible

Kjell Qvale announced the Jensen Interceptor Convertible on 22 March 1974 and it was intended that this car would rival the Rolls Royce Corniche. Although originally destined to be unveiled at the 1974 New York Motor Show, the Jensen Interceptor Convertible was in fact unveiled at the 1974 Geneva Motor Show.

Around five prototype Jensen Interceptor Convertibles were made and one of the early production cars, CEA 878N was used by Kevin Beattie.

One particular Jensen Interceptor Convertible, the unique ex-Dave Horton Convertible was specially built by Jensen Parts and Service. Registered VOR 604H it featured a tuned SP engine and an FF transmission unit.

Jensen Interceptor III Convertible	
1973	2 cars
1974	190 cars
1975	263 cars
1976	54 cars
Total	509 cars

Launched in March 1974, the Jensen Interceptor Convertible had the 7.2 Litre Chrysler V8.

This engine produced 330bhp and effortless performance.

Bore and stroke of the engine was 109·72mm x 95·25mm.

Specification
Front Engine, Rear-Wheel Drive

ENGINE

Cylinders	8, in 90 degree vee
Main bearings	5
Cooling system	Water; pump, thermostats and electric fans
Bore	109.72 mm (4.32 in)
Stroke	95.25 mm (3.75 in)
Displacement	7,212 cc (440 cu in)
Valve gear	Overhead, hydraulic tappets
Compression ratio	8.2 to 1. Min. octane rating: 91 RM
Carburettors	One Carter four choke
Fuel pump	Carter mechanical
Oil filter	Full flow, renewable element
Max. power	280 bhp (net) at 4,800 rpm
Max. torque	380 lb ft (net) at 3,200 rpm

TRANSMISSION

Gearbox	Chrysler Torqueflite 3-speed epicyclic with torque converter
Gear ratios	Top (auto) 1.0-2.0 Inter 1.45-2.90 Low 2.45-4.90 Reverse 2.2-4.4
Final drive	Salisbury hypoid bevel with Powr-Lok differential
Mph at 1,000 rpm in top gear	24.8

CHASSIS and BODY

Construction	Steel body welded to tubular steel frame

SUSPENSION

Front	Independent; coil springs, double wishbones, telescopic dampers, anti-roll bar
Rear	Live axle; half-elliptic leaf springs, Panhard rod, telescopic dampers

STEERING

Type	Adwest rack and pinion, with power assistance
Wheel diameter	15 in

BRAKES

Make and type	Girling ventilated discs front and rear. Divided hydraulic circuits
Servo	Girling vacuum
Dimensions	F, 10.75 in diameter R, 10.75 in diameter F, 208.5 sq in, R, 208.5 sq in Total 417 sq in (216 sq in/ton lader

WHEELS

Type	Cast aluminium alloy 6.5 in wide rim
Tyres - make	Dunlop
- type	Radial ply tubed
- size	ER70VR 15 in

EQUIPMENT

Battery	12 volt 66 Ah
Alternator	60 amp a.c.
Headlamps	Lucas 4-lamp 110/220 watt (total)
Reversing lamp	Standard
Electric fuses	12 + 10 in-line
Screen wipers	Two-speed, self-parking
Screen washer	Standard electric
Interior heater	Standard, air conditioning
Heated backlight	Not applicable
Safety belts	Standard, inertia reel
Interior trim	Leather seats, pvc headlining
Floor covering	Carpet
Jack	Bevel lift screw pillar
Jacking points	Two each side under sills
Windscreen	Laminated
Underbody protection	Bitumastic compound on surfaces exposed to road

MAINTENANCE

Fuel tank	20 Imp. Gallons (91 litres
Cooling system	32 pints (inc. heater)
Engine sump	8.5 pints (4.7 litres) SAE 20W/50. Change oil every 4000 miles. Change filter every 8000 miles
Gearbox	17 pints. ATF type A. No change
Final drive	3 pints. Shell l.s.d. oil S6721A Change every 8000 miles
Grease	4 points every 4000 miles
Valve clearance	Hydraulic (non-adjustable)
Ignition timing	10 deg. BTDC (static)
Spark plug	Type: Champion J11Y. Gap 0.035i
Compression pressure	100 psi.

Performance

ACCELERATION

True speed mph	Time in secs	Car Speedo mph
30	2.7	30
40	4.0	40
50	5.5	49
60	7.6	59
70	9.8	69
80	12.5	79
90	15.8	89
100	20.2	99
110	26.0	111
120	35.0	123

Standing ¼ mile
15.8 sec 90 mph

Standing kilometre
28.8 sec 113 mph

Mileage recorder:
3.5 per cent over-reading

GEARING
(with ER70 VR15in. tyres)

Top	24.8 mph per 1000 rpm
2nd	17.13 mph per 1000 rpm
1st	10.14 mph per 1000 rpm

MAXIMUM SPEED

Gear	mph	kph	rpm
Top (mean)	126	203	5100
(best)	126	203	5100
2nd	87	140	5100
1st	52	84	5100

BRAKES
FADE (from 70 mph in neutral)
Pedal load for 0.5g stops in lb

1	30	6	30-25
2	30-25	7	30-25
3	30-25	8	30-25
4	30-25	9	30-25
5	30-25	10	30-25

GEAR RATIOS AND TIME IN SEC

mph	Top (3.07 – 6.14)	2nd (4.44 – 8.88)	1st (7.50 – 15.0)
0-20	-	-	1.7
10-30	-	-	1.9
20-40	-	-	2.4
30-50	-	-	2.7
40-60	-	3.6	-
50-70	-	4.3	-
60-80	-	5.1	-
70-90	6.9	-	-
80-100	7.4	-	-
90-110	10.1	-	-
100-120	14.6	-	-

RESPONSE (from 30 mph in neutral)

Load	g	Distance
20lb	0.22	137 ft
40lb	0.65	46 ft
60lb	0.85	35 ft
80lb	0.91	33 ft
100lb	0.96	31.4 ft
Handbrake	0.35	86 ft
Max. gradient	1 in 4	

TURNING CIRCLES
Between kerbs
L, 37 ft 7 in.; R, 37 ft 2 in.
Between walls
L, 30 ft 4 in.; R, 38 ft 11 in.
Steering wheel turns, lock to lock 3.6

WEIGHT
Kerb weight 35.7 cwt (3997 lb – 1813 kg)
(with oil, water and half-full fuel tank)
Distribution per cent:
F, 51.8; R, 48.2
Laden as tested:
39.0 cwt (4372 lb – 1983 kg)

When sales of the Jensen Healey did not take off as had been hoped, Qvale made changes to suit the American market. With the Californian climate in mind he introduced the Jensen Interceptor Convertible in 1974.

The Jensen Interceptor Convertible sold well in the U.S., but it came too late in the Jensen Motors story. 1974 was the year that saw a major oil crisis and a sudden loss of interest in anything over 5 litres.

Convertibles are always beautifully upholstered.

Rear seats on this convertible are superb in tan.

Hood stowage creates a somewhat ungainly hump behind the rear seats.

Jensen Interceptor Convertible		
VIN Prefix Code	**Market Area**	**Numbers Built**
2340	Home	86
2320, 2321, 2323	Europe	5
2341	Australia	2
2342	Japan	1
2344	Hong Kong	2
2310, 2311	NADA	409
Figures exclude 4 prototype chassis	**TOTAL**	**505**

The four digit VIN prefix codes, above, of the Jensen Interceptor Convertible indicate which market they were destined for.

Here can be seen bumper overiders that were a feature of U.S.A. cars, the destination of the largest share of convertibles.

Above can be seen the air conditioning controls and the automatic shift on the Convertible's console.

Jensen Interceptor III

The Jensen Interceptor Mark III was launched with the Jensen Interceptor SP and the Jensen Interceptor FF III at Earl's Court in 1971.

For the Mark III there was a repositioning of the front number-plate which was now placed below the revised front bumper. At the back there was a single light to illuminate the number-plate and vents on the front wings now incorporated side indicators. Another change was that the headlights were set in black-painted cast-alloy surrounds.

Jensen's publicity photographs for the MK III showed it's eight-track stereo radio and padded steering wheel. The air-conditioning system was improved on the Jensen Interceptor MK III and central locking became standard.

Front ride height was raised by two inches on Jensen Interceptor SP's and Jensen Interceptor MK III's. Also on Mark III cars were GKN five-spoke alloys which meant that Jensen Interceptors could now have wider and more modern tyres. The Jensen Interceptor SP and Mark III models also had a new dual-circuit braking system.

After 1971, Jensen Interceptor Mark III and SP models got six and a half inch GKN alloy wheels which were a significant styling improvement.

Jensen Interceptor III 1971 - 1973				
Chassis Series	**Drive**	**Model**	**Jensen Series**	**Numbers Built**
128	RHD	Interceptor III	G and H	703
129	LHD	Interceptor III	G and H	15
133	LHD	Interceptor III	G, H, J	368
136	RHD	Interceptor III	J	735
140	LHD	Interceptor III	J	424
			TOTAL	**2477**

This Jensen Interceptor III is Chassis Number 2240/9417

Driving position in this Jensen Interceptor III

This Interceptor III has Engine Number 4C12353

Jensen SP (Six Pack)

The Jensen Interceptor SP was introduced in October 1971 to replace the Jensen Interceptor FF. SP stood for Six-Pack and was referring to the three twin-choke Holley carburettors that were found on the 7.2 Chrysler V8. This engine gave 330bhp.

The Jensen Interceptor SP had a vinyl roof and was the first car from Jensen to get a side indicator in the front wing air vent.

In order to cope with the considerably high heat output of the bigger 7.2 litre engine the bonnet louvres played an important part in helping to keep under-bonnet temperatures down.

The Jensen Interceptor SP has conventional design suspension with coil springs at the front and a live axle on leaf springs at the rear. Power assisted steering is standard using the Adwest rack and pinion system.

Electric window lifts are standard, with switches conveniently located either side of the transmission selector.

The Jensen Interceptor SP extends the range by serving as an additional model for those who are more concerned about performance than refinement. Extra acceleration from the Jensen Interceptor SP is somewhat marginal.

Jensen Interceptor SP Production Figures			
Chassis Series	**Drive**	**Engine Type**	**Numbers Built**
131	RHD	G and H Series	130
132	LHD	G and H Series	12
134	LHD	H Series	1
138	RHD	H Series	89
		Total Produced September 1971 - July 1973	**232**

Jensen SP (Six Pack)

Specification

Front Engine, Rear-Wheel Drive

ENGINE

Cylinders	8, in 90-degree vee
Main bearings	5
Cooling system	Water; pump, thermostat and twin electric fans
Bore	109.8 mm (4.32 in)
Stroke	95.5 mm (3.75 in)
Displacement	7212 cc (440 cu in)
Valve gear	Overhead, hydraulic tappets
Compression ratio	10.3-to-1 Min octane rating: 100
Carburettors	Three twin-choke holley
Fuel pump	Carter mechanical
Oil filter	Fram full-flow, renewable element
Max. power	330 bhp (net) at 4700 rpm
Max. torque	490 lb ft (gross) at 3200 rpm

TRANSMISSION

Gearbox	Chrysler Torqueflite Hi-performance 3-speed automatic with torque converter
Gear ratios	Top (auto) 1.0 Inter 1.45 Low 2.45 Reverse 2.2
Final drive	Hypoid bevel with Powr-Lok limited slip differential, 2.88 to 1

CHASSIS and BODY

Construction	Steel body welded to tubular steel frame

SUSPENSION

Front	Independent, double wishbones, coil springs, telescopic dampers and anti-roll bar
Rear	Live axle on dual rate semi-elliptic leaf springs, Panhard rod, telescopic dampers

STEERING

Type	Adwest rack and pinion, with power assistance
Wheel diameter	15 in

BRAKES

Make and type	Girling ventilated discs front and rear. Divided hydraulic circuits
Dimensions	F 10.75 in dia discs R 10.75 in dia discs
Swept area	F 208.5 sq in, R 208.5 sq in Total 417 sq in (214 sq in/ton laden)

WHEELS

Type	Cast aluminium alloy 6.5 in wide rim
Tyres - make	Pirelli
- type	Radial ply tubed
- size	GR70-15 in

EQUIPMENT

Battery	12 volt 67 Ah.
Alternator	60 amp a.c.
Headlamps	Lucas 4-lamp 110/220 watt (total) tungsten-halogen
Reversing lamp	2 standard
Electric fuses	12
Screen wipers	2-speed, self-parking
Screen washer	Standard, electric
Interior heater	Standard, water valve type
Air conditioning	Standard
Heated backlight	Standard
Safety belts	Standard
Interior trim	Leather seats, pvc headlining
Floor covering	Carpet
Jack	Bevelift
Jacking points	2 each side under sills
Windscreen	Laminated
Underbody protection	Bitumastic compound on all surfaces exposed to road

MAINTENANCE

Fuel tank	20 Imp gallons (no reserve) (91 litres)
Cooling system	32 pints (including heater)
Engine sump	8.5 pints (4.7 litres) SAE 20W/40 Change oil every 4000 miles, filter element every 8000 miles
Gearbox	17 pints SAE ATF A. No change needed
Final drive	3 pints Shell Limited Slip diff S6721A. Change every 12000 mls
Grease	4 points every 4000 miles
Tyre pressures	F 28; R 32 psi (normal driving) F 36; R 40 psi (over 110 mph)

Jensen SP (Six Pack)

Performance

ACCELERATION

True speed mph	Time in secs	Car Speedo mph
30	2.9	30
40	4.1	40
50	5.4	50
60	6.9	60
70	8.9	70
80	11.1	81
90	13.5	92
100	16.8	104
110	20.9	114
120	25.6	127
130	33.9	140
140		151

Standing ¼ mile
14.8 sec 94 mph

Standing kilometre
26.7 sec 121 mph

GEAR RATIOS AND TIME IN SEC

mph	Top (2.88)	Inter (4.16)	Low (7.05)
10-30	-	-	2.3
20-40	-	3.3	2.2
30-50	5.0	3.8	2.4
40-60	4.8	3.9	3.0
50-70	5.8	3.7	-
60-80	6.4	4.1	-
70-90	6.3	4.7	-
80-100	6.6	6.0	-
90-110	7.4	-	-
100-120	9.0	-	-
110-130	13.4	-	-

TURNING CIRCLES

Between kerbs
L, 37 ft 7 in.; R, 37 ft 2 in.
Between walls
L, 39 ft 4 in.; R, 38 ft 11 in.
Steering wheel turns, lock to lock 3.6

GEARING

(with ER70 VR15in. tyres)

Top	26.7 mph per 1000 rpm
Inter	18.5 mph per 1000 rpm
Low	10.9 mph per 1000 rpm

MAXIMUM SPEED

Gear	mph	kph	rpm
Top (mean)	143	230	5350
(best)	145	234	5430
2nd	99	159	5400
1st	59	95	5400

BRAKES

FADE (from 70 mph in neutral)
Pedal load for 0.5g stops in lb

1	30-25	6	30
2	30-25	7	30
3	30-25	8	30
4	30-25	9	32-30
5	30-25	10	35-32

RESPONSE (from 30 mph in neutral)

Load	g	Distance
20lb	0.25	120 ft
40lb	0.50	60 ft
60lb	0.74	41 ft
80lb	0.83	36 ft
100lb	0.92	32 ft
120lb	0.97	31 ft
140lb	1.02	29.9 ft
Handbrake	0.36	84 ft
Max. gradient	1 in 4	

WEIGHT

Kerb weight 35.1 cwt (3934 lb – 1783 kg)
(with oil, water and half-full fuel tank)
Distribution per cent:
F, 51.3; R, 48.7
Laden as tested:
39.0 cwt (4372 lb – 1981 kg)

Jensen FF

The Jensen FF was launched at the 1966 Earl's Court Motor Show. Richard Graves is quoted as saying that the FF was on different tooling to other Jensen Interceptors because it was four inches longer and therefore the front panels were different.

Graves also questioned whether the margins were there for although they sold it at a premium a lot of extra cost went into it. Car magazine voted the FF Car of the Year in 1967.

Jensen FF's could not be converted into left hand drive and therefore could not be sold in the U.S.

The Jensen FF's ability in adverse weather conditions was incredible and the FF could get from 0-60 mph in 7.4 seconds but the arrival of the top of the range Jensen Interceptor SP in October 1971 meant the end was in sight for the Jensen Interceptor FF. Only seventeen FF III's were produced.

It should be noted that the original Jensen FF was based on a C-V8 body. It was displayed at the 1965 London Motor Show but because of the introduction of the Touring designed Jensen Interceptor the car was never put into production. An FF test rig for developing a left hand drive version was made but no left hand drive FF was ever made.

Jensen FF

Performance

ACCELERATION

True speed mph	Time in secs	Car Speedo mph
30	3.1	31
40	4.4	42
50	6.2	52
60	8.4	63
70	10.8	73
80	13.8	83
90	17.5	94
100	22.5	104
110	28.2	115
120	37.2	126

Standing ¼ mile
15.9 sec 86 mph

Standing kilometre
29.3 sec 111 mph

Mileage recorder:
1.7 per cent over-reading

TEST CONDITIONS

Weather	Cloudy, fine
Wind	0-5 mph
Temperature	0 deg C (32 deg F)

MAXIMUM SPEED

Gear	mph	kph	rpm
Top (mean)	130	209	5,080
(best)	130	209	5,080
Intermediate	88	142	5,000
Low	52	84	5,000

BRAKES

FADE (from 30 mph in neutral)

Load	g	Distance
20lb	0.28	107ft
40lb	0.65	46ft
50lb	0.83	36ft
60lb	0.90	33.4ft
Handbrake	0.40	75ft
Max gradient	1 in 4	

GEAR RATIOS AND TIME IN SEC

mph	Top (3.07 – 6.76)	Inter (4.45 – 9.79)	Low (7.52 – 16.55)
10-30	-	-	2.2
20-40	-	-	2.6
30-50	4.8	3.8	3.2
40-60	5.6	3.8	-
50-70	6.3	4.6	-
60-80	6.9	5.0	-
70-90	7.3	5.5	-
80-100	8.3	6.5	-
90-110	10.7	-	-
100-120	15.1	-	-

FUEL CONSUMPTION
(at constant speed – mpg)

30 mph	21.9
40 mph	21.9
50 mph	20.6
60 mph	19.3
70 mph	16.6
80 mph	14.8
90 mph	13.1
100 mph	11.5

Typical mpg 14.0 (20.2 litres/100 km)
Overall mpg 13.6 (20.8 litres/100 km)

TURNING CIRCLES
Between kerbs
L, 39 ft 10 in.; R, 39 ft 4.5 in.
Between walls
L, 41 ft 8.5 in.; R, 41 ft 1 in.
Steering wheel turns, lock to lock 3.6

WEIGHT
Kerb weight 35.7 cwt (3981 lb – 1806 kg)
(with oil, water and half-full fuel tank)
Distribution per cent:
F, 52.5; R, 47.5
Laden as tested:
39.3 cwt (4403 lb – 1998 kg)

This Jensen FF belongs to motoring correspondent Ray Potter

Above, a Jensen FF at Cropredy Bridge Garage.

FF badging on the boot denotes this model is something a bit special.

Twin air-vents identify that this is an FF model. Other Jensen Interceptors had one broader vent.

Driving position in the Jensen FF.

Interior of the Jensen FF is solid and can last almost indefinitely with care.

Jensen FF has the early style interior.

Headlights are closer together on the FF than on the ordinary Interceptor.

The chassis number plate of this Jensen FF.

Luxurious Connelly hide in this Jensen FF.

The powerhouse of the Jensen Interceptor FF. It says Jensen on the rocker cover but the Chrysler V8 is an American engine.

Dunlop's Maxaret anti-lock brake system operates on the vacuum brake booster.

Harry Ferguson was a tractor manufacturer with an interest in vehicle safety and with Freddie Dixon the idea of making a car with four wheel drive was discussed. Tony Rolt was also interested in the idea and in 1950 Harry Ferguson Research was set up with Freddie Dixon and Tony Rolt joining as Directors.

An agreement was reached between Ferguson and Jensen allowing Jensen to use the four-wheel-drive Maxaret system in a Jensen Car. This agreement was reached in 1962 but it was the 1965 Motor Show when the Jensen four-wheel-drive was first seen. It was exhibited on the Jensen stand along with the Jensen P66. The four-wheel-drive unit in the drive line meant the length of the car had to be increased by around four inches which was achieved by adding an extra section of body from the windscreen forwards.

The Jensen FF was well received at the 1966 Motor Show but no sooner had Jensen put the FF into production than Jensen's Sales and Production department pointed out the car was too costly to make as much of it was peculiar to the FF. It had great publicity value and Tony Good had said "The FF was the car in the showroom window which sold the Interceptor in the basement." But with the number of people involved in making the FF this limited the number that could be made.

The FF eventually gave way to the Jensen Interceptor SP.

A rear view of the FF

Chassis plate of this FF

Driving position in the FF

This particular Jensen FF is chassis number 119 113.

Mark II Jensen FF's gained the same trim and upholstery changes as their two wheel counterparts.

A total of 107 Mark II FF's were produced.

The Jensen FF II, introduced in October 1969 was capable of 0-60mph in 8.1 seconds and had a top speed of 141mph.

Jensen FF I and FF II side by side.

Jensen FF III Chassis Numbers Models Built: 15 Produced: September 1971 to December 1971	
130/309	130/322
130/315	130/323
130/316	130/324
130/317	130/325
130/318	130/326
130/319	130/327
130/320	130/328
130/321	

Jensen FF III Engine Numbers Models Built: 15 Produced: September 1971 to December 1971	
3529/130E	3537/130E
3530/130E	3539/130E
3531/130E	3538/130E
3533/130E	3540/130E
3532/130E	3541/130E
3535/130E	3542/130E
3534/130E	3543/130E
3536/130E	

Another Jensen Interceptor being restored at Cropredy Bridge Garage.

Taken back to the body shell this Jensen Interceptor is in the process of being restored.

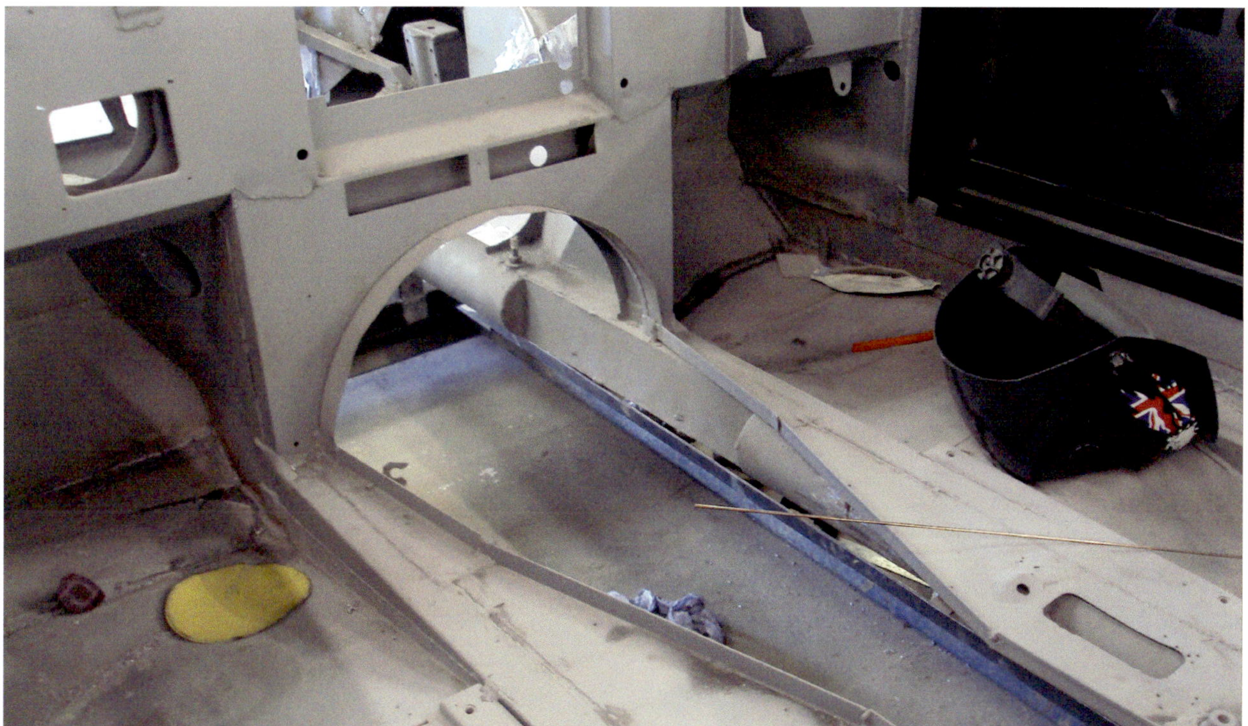

Originally a firm called V Eight re-invented the Jensen Interceptor with its Jensen Interceptor S.

Jensen Interceptor S Specifications	
Engine:	5967 cc V8 ohv, electronic fuel injection and engine management.
Power:	414 bhp @ 6000rpm.
Torque:	405 lb ft @ 4400 rpm.
Transmission:	Four-speed automatic with lock-up torque convertor, rear wheel drive and limited slip differential.
Brakes:	Vented discs front, discs rear.
Performance:	0-60 mph in 5.9 seconds.

Jensen Interceptor S badge on the boot signifies a car that has been given a fuel-injected 6 litre aluminium alloy General Motors LS2 V8. That is the engine used in the Chevrolet Corvette C6 of 2005 and the Vauxhall VXR8.

Jensen Interceptor S has 17 inch wheels with AP Racing Brakes as well as wire mesh side vents.

Jensen Interceptor S has 414 bhp as standard and is more powerful than the triple-carburettor Jensen Interceptor SP of 1971. But it returns around 20 mpg compared to 10-15 mpg for the Chrysler engine.

This Jensen Interceptor Coupe is Chassis 271/1961

This Coupe has the roof that was by Panther Cars

Interceptor Coupes with the non-Panther cars roof are very scarce

The roof and rear window of a Jensen Interceptor Coupe whose roof is not by Panther Cars

The rear window seen from inside on this Jensen Interceptor Coupe

Contrast the roof of this Jensen Interceptor Coupe that has the Panther Cars roof with those above

Below can be seen the interior of this rare Interceptor Coupe

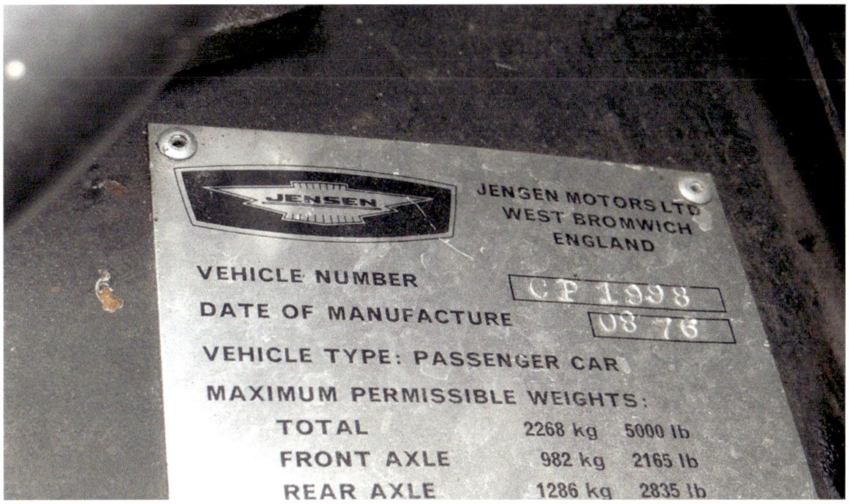

Chassis CP 1998 is the vehicle number of this Interceptor Coupe

Chassis CP 1998 has a double chrome bumper

Panther-cars roofed Coupe has double chrome bumper only for some of its width

This Jensen Interceptor Coupe has chassis number 2740/1863

All but one Jensen Interceptor Coupes were manufactured in 1976

Luxurious interior of the Jensen Interceptor Coupe.

Driving position on the Jensen Interceptor Coupe.

Jensen Interceptor Coupe had a walnut glove box.

Rear seats in the Jensen Interceptor

"J" in centre of the steering wheel.

"Coupe" badge on the rear wing.

All Jensen Interceptor Coupes had the Chrysler 440 ci V8 engine.

Jensen Interceptor Coupe		
Chassis Number	**Engine Number**	**Colour**
PT 1 - 75	(Experimental Car)	Yellow
2711/1716	–	Nevis Blue
2740/1850	5C00136	Sebring Silver
2740/1851	5C00188	Sebring Silver
2741/1852	5C00173	Pine Green
2740/1853	5C00175	Nevis Blue
2740/1854	–	Nevis Blue
2740/1855	–	Aruba Red
2740/1856	5C00224J	Saba Blue
2740/1857	5C00216	White

Jensen Interceptor Coupe		
Chassis Number	**Engine Number**	**Colour**
2740/1858	5C00206	Saba Blue
2740/1859	5C00193	Sebring Silver
2740/1860	5C00251J	Sebring Silver
2740/1861	–	Nevis Blue
2740/1862	(Tony Good's Car PHA 791R)	Pine Green
2740/1863	5C00431	Grey
2740/1866	–	Grey
2740/1866	–	Aruba Red
2740/1867	5C00406	Black
2740/1868	–	Saturn Gold
2740/1869	–	White

Jensen Interceptor Coupe		
Chassis Number	**Engine Number**	**Colour**
2740/1870	–	Nevis Blue
2740/1908	–	Pine Green
2740/1909	–	Saba Blue
2740/1910	5C00245J	Saturn Gold
271/1915	–	White
271/1916	–	–
271/1960	–	Silver Grey
271/1961	(Registered RGN602P)	Nevis Blue
271/1962	–	Black
2710/1965	–	Aruba Red

Jensen Interceptor Coupe		
Chassis Number	**Engine Number**	**Colour**
2711/1968	–	Cheviot Brown
271/1971	–	Nevis Blue
2711/1974	–	Saturn Gold
271/1977	–	–
2711/1978	–	Saba Blue
271/1981	–	Black
271/1983	–	White
271/1988	–	Nevis Blue
2711/1989	5C00269	White
271/1990	–	White

Chassis plate of the Jensen Interceptor Coupe

Panther Cars Ltd was contracted to design and build the special roofs.

Jensen Interceptor R

In May 2010, Jensen International Automotive was set up with the financial backing of Carphone Warehouse founder Charles Dunstone. A small number of Jensen Interceptor S's which were started under V Eight are being completed by Jensen International Automotive in parallel with Jensens International Automotive's own production of the new Jensen Interceptor R.

The Jensen Interceptor was always a luxury car, but was never this sumptuously finished.

A GM 4L70 E 4-Speed Automatic gearbox is used on the Jensen Interceptor R. The Final Drive has limited slip differential.

The General Motors LS3 V8-engine delivers 429 bhp, through either a 4-speed automatic or 6-speed manual gearbox.

This is the even more powerful Jensen Interceptor R with a supercharger.

Badge denotes this is the supercharged version of the Interceptor R.

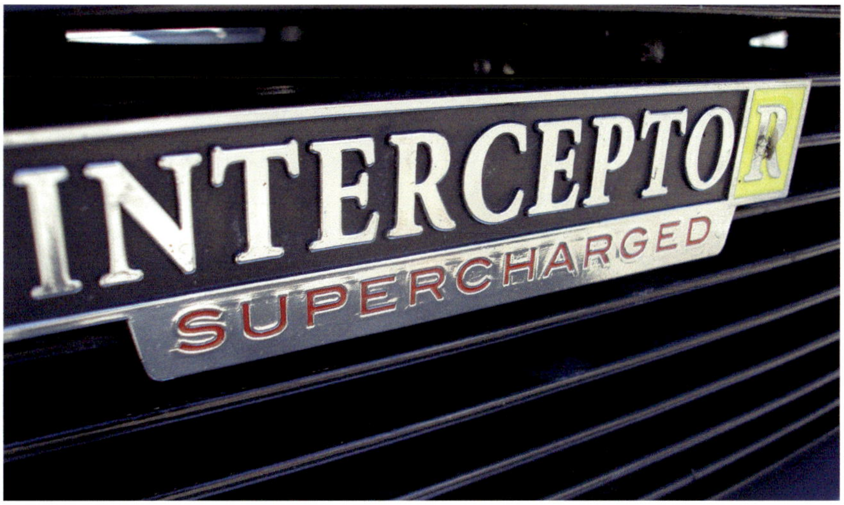

Instrumentation of the supercharged Interceptor R.

Sumptuous finish on rear seats with double stitched seams and cross-hatching.

Supercharged Jensen Interceptor R has over 600 bhp.

New propshaft to suit fully independent rear suspension system with single lower wishbone and stressed driveshaft as upper link is fitted by JIA.

NOA 369P was built by Jensen for display at the 1976 Irish Motor Show.

The Interceptor above is seen here outside Cropredy Bridge Garage's workshops

Jensen Interceptor I (RHD)			
Chassis Number	**Engine Number**	**Colour**	**Significance**
117/2500	507/17B	Crystal Blue	The Turin Motor Show Car for November 1966
117/2501	544/17B	Charcoal Grey	The Geneva Motor Show Car for March 1967
115/2515	509/15V	Crystal Blue	Earl's Court Motor Show Car for 1966
115/2516	503/15V (HEA 2D)	Regal Red	Earl's Court Motor Show Car for 1966
115/2667	731/15B	Charcoal Grey	Earl's Court Motor Show Car for 1967
115/2700	734/15B	Stratosphere Blue	Earl's Court Motor Show Car for 1967
118/2860	890/18A	Flag Red	Paris Motor Show Car for 1968
117/3130	1136/17D	White	Paris Motor Show Car for 1968

Jensen Interceptor I (RHD)			
Chassis Number	**Engine Number**	**Colour**	**Significance**
117/3137	1324/17D	Flag Red	Brussel's Motor Show Car for 1969
117/3138	1330/17D	Moorland Peat	Brussel's Motor Show Car for 1969
Jensen Interceptor FFI			
119/018	681/19B (NEA 4F)	Metallic Peat	Earl's Court Motor Show Car for 1967
119/025	680/19B	Stratosphere Blue	Earl's Court Motor Show Car for 1967
119/081	1160/19D	Stratosphere Blue	Earl's Court Motor Show Car for 1968
Jensen Interceptor FFII			
127/202	1825/127E	Beluga	Earl's Court Motor Show Car for 1969

Jensen Interceptor II (RHD)			
Chassis Number	**Engine Number**	**Colour**	**Significance**
123/3559	1812/123E	Metallic Quartz	Earl's Court Motor Show Car for 1969
123/3599	1853/123E	Pistachio	Scottish Motor Show Car for 1969
123/3636	1907/123E	Pimpernel	Melbourne Motor Show Car for 1970
123/3892	3287/123E	Silver Grey	Belfast Motor Show Car for 1971
123/3901	3302/123E	Yellow	Earl's Court Motor Show Car for 1970
123/3913	3310/123E	Berkeley Brown	Earl's Court Motor Show Car for 1970
Jensen Interceptor II (LHD)			
125/5001	1817/125E	Beluga	Paris Motor Show Car for 1969
125/5002	1830/125E	White	EC Motor Show Car for 1969

Jensen Interceptor II (LHD)			
Chassis Number	**Engine Number**	**Colour**	**Significance**
125/5015	1967/125E	Royal Flag Blue	Brussel's Motor Show Car for 1970
125/5024	2011/125E	Silver Grey	Geneva Motor Show Car for 1970
125/5025	3032/125E	Metallic Fawn	Geneva Motor Show Car for 1970
125/5026	3007/125F	Metallic Fawn	Barcelona Motor Show Car for 1970
125/5027	3049/125F	Mango	New York Motor Show Car for 1970
125/5108	J1072/125F	Reef Blue	Earl's Court Motor Show Car for 1970
125/5202	3464/125E	California Sage	Brussel's Motor Show Car for 1971
125/5244	3469/125E	Silver Grey	Geneva Motor Show Car for 1972

Jensen Interceptor III (LHD)			
Chassis Number	**Engine Number**	**Colour**	**Significance**
129/5655	JC1-218/129	White	Geneva Motor Show Car for 1972
132/5663	HC10148/132	Mustard	Barcelona Motor Show Car for 1972
Jensen Interceptor III (RHD)			
128/4266	J2497/128G	Mustard	Earl's Court Motor Show Car for 1971
128/4524	J2843/128G	Brasilia	Ulster Motor Show Car for 1972
140/8901	3C11630/140	Tangerine	Frankfurt Motor Show Car for 1973
140/8968	3C11901/140	White	Earl's Court Motor Show Car for 1973
136/9031	3C11966/136	Copper Red	Earl's Court Motor Show Car for 1973